This edition copyright © 2002 Lion Publishing

Published by
Lion Publishing plc
Mayfield House, 256 Banbury Road,
Oxford OX2 7DH, England
www.lion-publishing.co.uk
ISBN 0 7459 4800 6

First edition 2002
1 3 5 7 9 10 8 6 4 2 0

Picture acknowledgments

Picture research by Zooid Pictures Limited.

7: Michael Freeman/Corbis UK Ltd. 8: George Lee White/Corbis UK Ltd.
11: Wolfgang Kaehler/Corbis UK Ltd. 12: Gunter Marx/Corbis UK Ltd.
15: Gerrit Greve/Corbis UK Ltd. 16/17: Wolfgang Kaehler/Corbis UK Ltd.
19: Austrian Archives/Corbis UK Ltd. 20: Joseph Sohm/ChromoSohm Inc./
Corbis UK Ltd. 23: Gerrit Greve/Corbis UK Ltd. 25: Darwin Wiggett/Corbis UK Ltd.
27: Christie's Images/Corbis UK Ltd. 29: Yann Arthus-Bertrand/Corbis UK Ltd.

Text acknowledgments

6: George Macdonald. 9: Emanuel Swedenborg. 10: Author unknown.
13: William Hazlitt. 14: Antoine de Saint-Exupéry. 16/17: Oscar Wilde.
18: John Lennon. 20/21: Marcel Proust. 22/23: George Herbert. 24/25, 28:
1 Corinthians 13:4, 7, Song of Songs 8:7, taken from the Holy Bible,
New International Version, copyright © 1973, 1978, 1984 by International
Bible Society. Used by permission. 26: Jean Anouilh.

A catalogue record for this book is available
from the British Library

Typeset in Novarese
Printed and bound in Singapore

love

in words and images

LION
Giftlines

Love

makes

everything

lovely.

Love in its essence
is spiritual fire.

So

much

of what

we

know

of love

we

learn

at

home.

Love
    and joy
        are twins,
    or born
    of each
        other.

It is only with the heart that one can see rightly;

what is essential is invisible to the eye.

Keep love in your heart. A life without it

_ is like a sunless garden when the flowers are dead.

Love is like

a precious plant.

You've got to keep

watering it.

Les us be grateful to people who make us happy.

they are
the charming
gardeners who
make our souls
blossom.

Love makes
all hard hearts

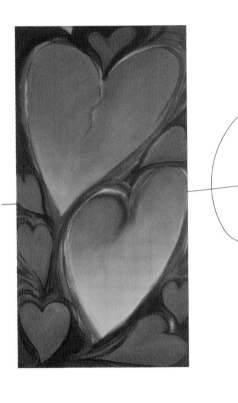

gentle.

Love is patient, love is kind.

It always protects,

always trusts,

always hopes,

always perseveres.

Love is, above all,

the gift of oneself.

Many waters
cannot quench love;
rivers cannot wash it away.

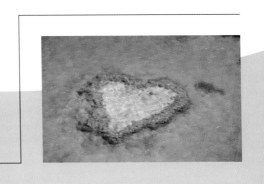